SISKIYOU COUNTY SCHOOLS
SCIENCE PROJECT

SISKIYOU COUNTY SCHOOLS
SCIENCE PROJECT

Teeth

SISKIYOU COUNTY SCHOOLS
SCIENCE PROJECT

WONDER
STARTERS

Teeth

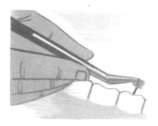

Pictures by MICHAEL RICKETTS

35658

Published by WONDER BOOKS
A Division of Grosset & Dunlap, Inc.

51 Madison Avenue   New York, N.Y. 10010

About Wonder Starters

Wonder Starters are vocabulary controlled information books for young children. More than ninety per cent of the words in the text will be in the reading vocabulary of the vast majority of young readers. Word and sentence length have also been carefully controlled.

Key new words associated with the topic of each book are repeated with picture explanations in the Starters dictionary at the end. The dictionary can also be used as an index for teaching children to look things up.

Teachers and experts have been consulted on the content and accuracy of the books.

Published in the United States by Wonder Books, a Division of Grosset & Dunlap, Inc.

ISBN: 0-448-09654-4 (Trade Edition)
ISBN: 0-448-06374-3 (Library Edition)

FIRST PRINTING 1972

Printed and bound in the United States.

My tooth is wobbly.
It will come out soon.

1

A new tooth is growing.
It is pushing my old tooth out.
2

The old tooth has come out now.
There is a gap in my teeth.
The new tooth grows slowly.

Sweet food can make teeth bad.
There is sugar in sweet foods.
Sugar is bad for teeth.

4

Food sticks in teeth.
Some bits of food go bad.

Keep teeth clean with a toothbrush.
The toothbrush brushes away food
and dirt.
6

Apples help keep teeth clean.
Carrots are good for teeth, too.

My tooth hurts.
I have a toothache.
I must go to the dentist.

The dentist looks into my mouth.
He can see a bad tooth.

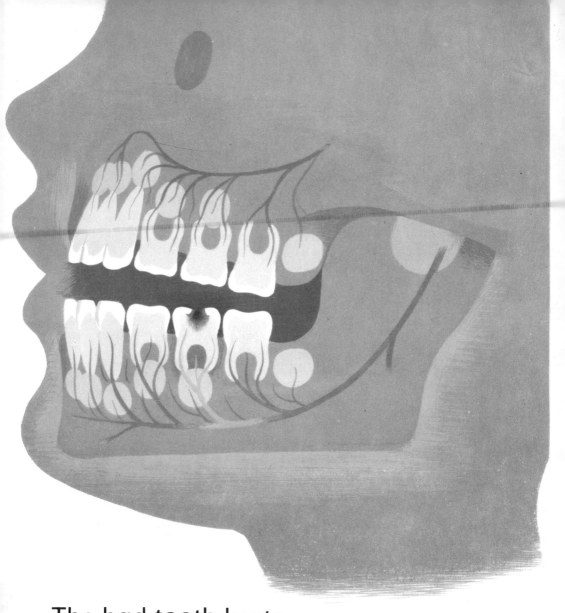

The bad tooth hurts.
A nerve goes from the tooth to the jaw.
The pain goes down the nerve.

The dentist drills the bad part away.
Now there is a hole.

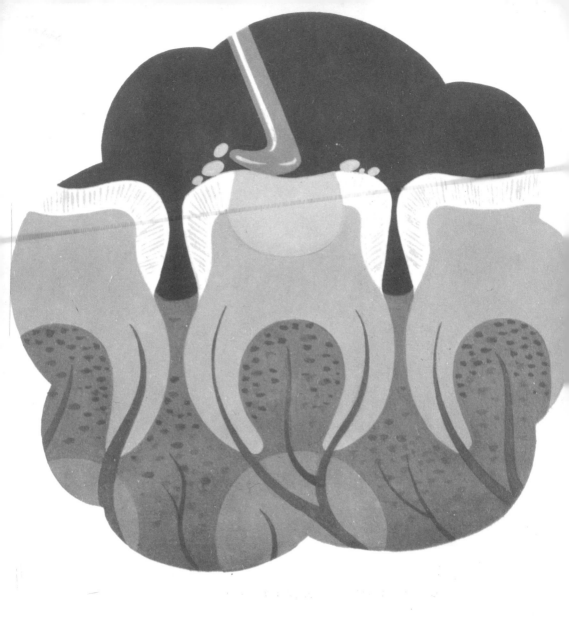

The dentist puts a filling in the hole.
Now the tooth is good again.
12

Teeth have different shapes.
Front teeth are sharp.
Back teeth are flat.

13

Animals that eat meat
have sharp teeth.
These animals eat meat.
Look at their sharp teeth.
14

shark

barracuda

skull of barracuda

angler fish

These fishes eat other fishes.
They have sharp teeth, too.

15

skull of cow

Cows eat grass.
Their teeth are flatter.
The flat teeth chew the grass.
16

deer

sheep

giraffe

These animals eat grass and plants.
Their teeth are mostly flat.

17

Elephants have two very long teeth.
These are called tusks.
Elephants have smaller teeth, too.

Some snakes have poison teeth.
Rattlesnakes have poison teeth.
They can hurt people and animals.

The walrus has tusks.
He digs out shells with his tusks.

Some animals gnaw wood.
Beavers gnaw trees down.
Mice gnaw holes in wood.
These animals are rodents.

See for yourself.
Here are the jawbones
of two dinosaurs.
Which ate meat?   Which ate plants?
22

Starter's **Teeth** words

tooth
(page 1)

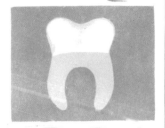

gap
(page 3)

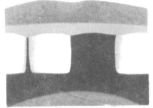

tooth-
brush
(page 6)

apple
(page 7)

carrot
(page 7)

dentist
(page 8)

mouth
(page 9)

nerve
(page 10)

jaw
(page 10)

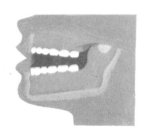

drill
(page 11)

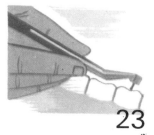

23

shark
(page 15)

barra-
cuda
(page 15)

giraffe
(page 17)

deer
(page 17)

tusk
(page 18)

rattle-
snake
(page 19)

walrus
(page 20)

gnaw
(page 21)

beaver
(page 21)

dinosaur
(page 22)

SISKIYOU COUNTY SCHOOLS
SCIENCE PROJECT

SISKIYOU COUNTY SCHOOLS
SCIENCE PROJECT